AN AMERICAN TRAGEDY

How Race Defined And Defiled

Our Nations History

DR. L. RONALD DURHAM

Publisher Information:
Independently Published
P.O. Box 1773
Daytona Beach, FL. 32115
2019
United States of America
Cover design by
Copyright @ 2019 by Rev. Dr. L. Ronald Durham
ISBN: 9781096514633

CONTENTS

INTRODUCTION

It was ambition, greed and the quest for wealth and power that led to worldwide slavery and our present day concept of race color and racism. This ambition created an ideology of racial difference between White and Black people based on the word race and the color of our skin. Which has divided America into two societies, one White and one, Black. One living the American Dream, while the other existing in its nightmare. It was this divisive racial attitude that triggered an American culture and tradition of legalized Slavery, Segregation, Jim Crow Laws, traditional racial discrimination, hatred and disrespect in America and worldwide against Black People that has lasted for over 393 years, to the present day racist attitudes.

We have abolished the evil institution of slavery, Segregation and Jim Crow Laws. We have passed numerous laws making racial discrimination a crime and act of violence against other people because of their race, a hate crime. But we have not abolished the concept of race from our social consciousness or even investigated whether or not the concept of race is really true. Because we still require our citizens to identify themselves according to race. The racist attitudes that cause some of us to commit acts of racial discrimination and hate crimes are still alive because we have failed as a society and as individuals to adequately educate ourselves to deal with the truth about the false concept of race based on skin color. Because of this failure, we have allowed race to become institutionalized in our hearts and minds. As a result, some people are still committing racially motivated hate crimes because of their belief in the false concept of race and the seeds of hatred it has planted in their Souls. The concept of the word race as it is defined in our society is the social, racial difference between Black and White People based on the color of their skin, and ancestry bloodline.....

HAS RACISM AND BIGOTRY BEEN REPACKAGED IN AMERICA

It's Time We Stop Ignoring Racism in America. Racism has obviously disguised itself in a variety of ways. One of Racism's many personalities allows it to masquerade as justice. This is perhaps the deadliest weapon in violating African American rights. The deaths of Sandra Bland and Trayvon Martin are prime examples of how dangerous race tactics are when placed in the hands of unfair law enforcement. Racially charged killings by authorities are at an all time high and the hatred that rears its ugly head from behind a Patriotic mask has Americans chanting, "Go back to Mexico!" to other Americans. We never see what race the Monster is from behind its red, white and blue veil. Make America Great Again? Nobody ever told me that America had to be a certain color to be great?

Social commentary has been reduced to crude jokes and stereotypes? The media is not taking it seriously enough that there's been no reparations made on behalf of the Government to people of color. Is the whole country laughing in the face of Black America? What is even more

Surprising is that we don't believe African Americans should be angry. We forget that Segregation was still legal 54 years ago after a dreadful 400 years of slavery and America revisits this hell on earth every Black History Month. These images replay themselves in the minds of a slave's descendent every time it's talked about. Old wounds are reopened every time an African American is done an injustice. It's been a long time coming but it will take twice as long to heal. On the flip side White Americans are made to feel guilty and tired of having to proceed with caution around a person of color'. Images in pop culture suggest that Blacks are violent criminals, angering them is the last thing anyone wants to do but everyone has pride. I understand slavery was not your fault but the fact that the past is hurting our present is proof that America must deal with the sins of its forefathers. If we don't, then the future will be divided. It's Time We Stop Ignoring Racism In America before unspoken words become actions.

In American society, issues of race and social class are entwined together like a chain of DNA. One cannot have an honest discussion about race without looking at the equally important issue of class since the two are closely linked. Although discussions of race and class are often avoided because these type of issues make people uncomfortable, Hurricane Katrina and the various television newscasts that followed stripped away the curtain to America's dirty little secret: there are many people in American society who have been unable to escape the double jeopardy of being born African American and poor.

RACIAL AND ETHNIC PROFILING

Prejudice: Unfavorable opinion or feeling formed beforehand without knowledge, thought or reason.
Profiling: Unfavorable targeting people based on ethnic or nationality.

Racial and ethnic profiling is the use of race or ethnicity either as the sole factor, or as one factor among many, in a decision to detain or arrest an individual, or to subject an individual to heightened scrutiny or investigation. Whether used as the sole factor, or one factor along with others (e.g. suspect behavior), profiling allows race or ethnicity to play a determinative factor in investigative decisions allowing distinctions to be drawn among otherwise identical persons on the basis of race or ethnicity.

Profiling employs race and ethnicity as a proxy for the risk of committing criminal acts. But to profile in this way raises the serious danger of tarring an entire group with the crimes of the few, by giving rise to the myth that being a member of a certain racial or ethnic group reflects a propensity to engage in criminal activity. It would also be significant that profiling would occur in the context of law enforcement, where the goal is to identify those who pose a threat of engaging in criminal activity. The mere fact of being subject to investigation in the criminal context carries with it a stigma.

For the persons who are profiled, the indignity is real. In essence, profiling requires them to establish their legitimacy to the satisfaction of state officials. The cumulative effect on individuals of bearing this burden, simply because of their looks, would be enormously damaging on their self-respect.

It would also undermine fundamental principles of equal dignity and worth and respect for the presumption of innocence.

Ethnic profiling is the practice of identifying suspects based on their physical appearance, which violates civil liberties and will ultimately prove ineffective at fighting terrorism. Innocent people have been killed and guilty ones allowed going free because officials based their decisions on the suspects' physical characteristics. Since a person's appearance does not always convey his or her intention of committing a wrongful act, ethnic profiling will ultimately fail to identify terrorists.

Race: Race is a group of individuals who share common physical characteristics, history, nationality and geographic location. Race characterizes individuals based on physical appearance, and infers stereotyped differences between individuals. Ethnicity overlaps race, and represents cultural and historical differences. Biological aspect of race, where genes determine skin color and physical characteristics, are inherited. On the other side of the debate, there are no universal characteristics among all or even most individuals of the same race or characteristics that one race has that another does not have.

Racism: Any attitude, action or institutional structure which subordinates a person or group because of their color. Racism is not just a matter of attitudes: actions and institutional structures can also be a racism.

Racism is different from racial prejudice, hatred, or discrimination. Racism involved having power to carry out systematic discriminatory practices through major institution of the society. When you combine power with racial discrimination the result is racism. And racism is not how you look, rather it is how people assign meaning to how you look and sound.

<u>Racial Discrimination</u>: Any distinction, exclusion, restriction or preference based on race, color, descent, or national or ethnic origin which has the purpose or effect of nullifying or impairing the recognition, enjoyment or exercise, on an equal footing, of human rights and fundamental freedoms in the political, economic, social, cultural and any other field of public life. Racial discrimination is racism in action.

Racism = Power + Prejudice

In the America at present, only whites can be racists, since whites dominate and control the institutions that create and enforce American cultural norms and values, blacks, and other minorities do not have the access to the power to enforce and prejudices they may have, so they can not by definition, be racists.

Racism is a critical and pervasive form of mental illness. Racism has all the classic element of destructive behavior including acting out, denial of reality, projection, transference of blame, disassociation and justification.

The delusion of white superiority manifested itself as arrogance, coupled with a disdain for everything that is non-white. This perpetuated by the deliberate omission, falsification and emphasis, leading to a belief that everything great that was ever done was the work of whites.

Read the history books of the ancient world and you will be surprised by the developments and advancements from the other parts of the world.

BLACK RECONSTRUCTION

Reconstruction was America's first experiment in interracial democracy for men. It tested the central philosophies and traditions of America's society and institutions. The Civil War entailed a dramatic expansion of the roles and responsibilities of the central government that resulted in the ratification of the Thirteenth, Fourteenth, and Fifteenth Amendments to the Constitution. These amendments made involuntary servitude a federal crime, created a new federal dimension of citizenship for all Americans, and sought to guarantee universal male suffrage. Once they were ratified, Congress was constitutionally empowered and obligated to protect and enforce them, sustaining the broad new powers and active role of the national government.

The postwar period began with a series of fairly lenient Reconstruction plans put forth by presidents Lincoln and Johnson, who were both eager to see the former Confederacy returned to the Union with as much speed and as little vindictiveness as possible. As the ineffectiveness of

Presidential Reconstruction became apparent in the face of blatant violations of the freed peoples' constitutional rights and liberties, northern voters elected Republicans to Congress by a landslide, thereby providing a mandate for the Republicans to take over the job of putting the Union back together again. They were deemed "radical" by subsequent historians because they insisted that blacks be protected in their newfound rights.

When white southern intransigence followed the nation's first Civil Rights Act, Congress passed the Ku Klux Klan Act , which gave federal authorities jurisdiction over both states and individuals who tried to deprive freedmen and women of their newfound rights. Never before had the federal government intervened so forcefully and directly on behalf of its citizens, let alone its most castigated and impoverished minority.

Yet even that unprecedented level of involvement proved insufficient to protect African-Americans or bring about a fundamental change in racial attitudes. Not since the Haitian Revolution had a recently enslaved population risen up amidst cataclysmic social change to claim their own rights and freedoms, to exercise power at every level of government in a society that had been—and, to a great extent, remained—predicated upon the concept of white supremacy. Central to the struggle of the emancipated men and women was the question, "How free is free?" Was freedom simply the absence of bondage, or the right to obtain an education, to receive healthcare, to negotiate for wages, to vote, and to tend one's own plot of land?

Black scholar W.E.B. Du Bois, who was born in 1868—the year that the Fourteenth Amendment was ratified—famously termed the Reconstruction period a "splendid failure," for it did not fail for the reasons that whites thought or expected that it would. Rather than revealing any innate inferiority or incompetence, some 2,000 black Americans governed reasonably well in nearly every level of government, from the Senate to the local sheriff and tax collector. They learned the uses of political power and served with great courage amidst a hostile environment of embittered and war-scared southern whites, many of whom targeted black representatives with violent attacks.

During Reconstruction, African-Americans formed their own fraternal organizations and worshipped in their own churches, and they embraced the notion of an activist government that promoted and safeguarded the welfare of its citizens. Rather than becoming the illiterate, ignorant dupes of demagogues and northern white Republicans, as so many whites suspected or believed, black men and women eagerly obtained the education that had been denied them by law under slavery. The Reconstruction governments were hardly perfect, but blacks proved themselves neither superior nor inferior to their white counterparts. This in itself was a revolutionary concept, in a society were white supremacy remained the central tenet of life, North and South, and where white ministers preached from the pulpit on Sundays that blacks had descended from Ham, and were therefore an inferior race, separated from the superior Anglo Saxon (even though the Curse of Ham passage in the Book of Genesis makes no mention of skin color or race).

Corruption and bribery did take place in government during Reconstruction, as they had prior to the Civil War and as they still do today. Railroad promoters, business speculators and their retainers, land contractors, and stock market investors all sought to purchase their share of influence with elected leaders. As one black representative and former slave commented, "I've been sold eleven times in my life; this is the first time I ever got the money." Yet despite these moral frailties, all of the southern governments combined did not steal as much from the public treasury as William "Boss" Tweed's Ring in New York City, a Democratic Party machine that lined its pockets with over $75 million, or the Republican "Gas Ring" in Philadelphia , which did the same thing. Though such comparisons do not excuse the failings that Reconstruction governments did exhibit, the fact remains that such governments did establish some of the first public and social services in the South outside of North Carolina; they collected taxes to fund public schools, expand hospitals, and build asylums, among other programs.

Nonetheless, as whites regained power over the South by 1877 and throughout the century that followed, whites from both North and South pilloried the Reconstruction period as a disaster because blacks were in charge, and were—by their interpretation—racially unfit to rule and unprepared for the rights, responsibilities, and freedoms granted to them in postwar America. Reconstruction-era instances of corruption or bribery were vastly exaggerated; the nation's foremost scholars, especially historians, wrote seething histories of the period that decried the supposedly deplorable treatment of white southerners and spun overtly racist tales concerning the ignorance and savage lust of black officeholders. The two sides of the Civil War reunited during the late nineteenth century by casting the fate of the black population aside and basing innumerable aspects of their reunited culture, education, and society on the concept of white supremacy.In fact, whites during Reconstruction had responded the same way to all Reconstruction governments, whether corrupt or not. The white South turned to force to end the country's first experiment in integrated govern-ment; not because of black failure, but because of black success. Evidence of black ambition, confidence, and aptitude threatened the power structure, institutions, labor system, and society of the former Confederacy more than black corruption or ignorance ever could. But by discrediting the era in which blacks were most active politically, historians, filmmakers, politicians, and writers from across the country effectively acquitted the white South of disfranchising blacks under the Redemption and Jim Crow periods; they permitted racial segregation and discrimination, and even sanctioned it, for over a century.

SUBURNIZATION SEGREGATION

In the 1950's and 60's boom, the suburbs exploded. Through this explosion of outskirt city living, a huge racial divide increased to a whole other level by several factors including zoning ordinances, home sales practices, bank lending policies, etc. This suppression significantly favored middle and upper class white people and prevented people of color from leaving the cities. A majority of individuals are unaware of this tragedy as it is a much subtler form of suppression due to its many factors with many more behind the scene acts of discrimination compared to blatant racism exemplified in Jim Crow laws. Housing discrimination has always been an issue and unfortunately it still is today. With immoral acts from the government, banks, and real estate organizations, people of color have been targeted and cheated especially in the suburbanization of the 50's and 60's.

Government Suppression

The government housing segregation was the sum of immoral decisions over time. An example of this was the Federal Housing Act of 1949. In response to the lack of housing across the nation, Harry Truman and the legislative branch passed a bill to increase the amount of homes. Decent in thought, however, with poor planning and racist America, more homes were torn down than built.

Primarily of course, minority slums brought down and replaced with much higher income housing or public commodities that did not support the past minority population. All over the country the Conservative outlook which was against housing, defeated any attempts to build low rent housing displacing primarily black families from temporary war housing into overcrowded black neighborhoods which eventually expanded into new all black neighborhoods. This was the case for the east bay in

California and is the main culprit as to why Berkeley, Oakland, and Richmond, became rigidly segregated communities. The government made policies that offered low cost financing to millions of people. Another program developed by the government was called The Veteran's Mortgage Guarantee program. With a very small amount of money down and low monthly payments, huge numbers of people were able to buy houses in the suburbs. However, this money was only available to white people. This low cost opportunity led to thousands of white people fleeing the city in what is now known as the "white flight." With the loss of clientele, businesses had to resort to following the fleeing population leaving people of color in the "ghettos" of urbanization. The image portrayed here is that suburbanization uprising had to do a lot more than limited housing, it absolutely crippled job opportunities and the employment level for people of color. With Jobs sprawling out to the suburbs to follow the money, people in the city had to commute even if they somehow did pull of finding a job.

The large job growth in the suburbs directly correlates for the racial difference in youth unemployment rates. With yet another economic disadvantage, it made the middle class vision and the possibility of living in the suburbs impossible for people of color. The investments in public funding shifted toward the suburbs. This flux of not only private businesses but public sector funding benefited the white middle class. Public policies and private investment decisions increased the number of impoverished black neighborhoods in cities by moving all the economic growth from the cities to the suburbs. Luxuries from businesses to quality of schools were deeply affected directly contributing to higher levels of black and white residential segregation.

Whites continued to find ways such as racial zoning ordinances, racially restrictive covenants, urban renewal, and block busting, along with raw violence, as methods of restricting blacks from residing in white areas.

Another horrific example of governmental interference with people of color's right to the pursuit of happiness was the Federal Housing Administration. The Federal Housing Administration adopted the practice of redlining which was a discriminatory rating system used to evaluate the risks associated with loans made to borrowers in specific neighborhoods. Through right wing politics there is always implied criticism of people of color being unemployed as an education issue, in poverty because of laziness, and prevalent to crime because of culture which is such a negligent perspective and utterly racist. The ghettos exist because of this fought for prejudice exclusion that happened in the 50's. The American government and society literally forced people of color to live in poverty and result to crime.

Now today, people have forgotten what happened just 50 years ago and have somehow come up with the ideology that people of color have had the same opportunities as white people. As seen in this paragraph, the government was deliberately against people of color; same playing field? Absolutely not.

Private Sector Discrimination

Private discrimination amongst homeowners, realtors, and bankers account for a substantial amount of the suburbanization tragedy that occurred in the 50's as well as today. It was found that realtors would show people of color to houses away from white neighborhoods to ensure segregation. This was known as "steering" which is still prominent today as recent studies have shown. This was only amplified by landlords who would claim (and still do) the apartment has been taken off the market or demand an unreasonably large deposit or promise to put their name on a waiting list that never end.

Cities planned suburban developments with low tax incentives for builders and perspective industries. Real estate associations, conservative city planners and the federal government housing policies excluded minorities in order to maximize property values. All it took was a negative perspective and prejudice mindset from white society to really make it difficult to find a home, a job, and simply feel human. Local banks also sided to discriminate. Banks would refuse to approve mortgages for minorities making it impossible to afford a reasonable place outside of the ghettos in the city.

The sickening part of these findings is there are several examples of them occurring well into the 90's and into today, and when we begin to talk about women, the struggle only multiples with even less opportunities of success. White people have confided people of color to a place where economic growth is nonexistent causing a spiral affect with poor education and housing which leads to poor jobs, if any, forcing people of color to live in poverty and resorting to crime because there is no way out.

On the whole, suburbanization was another way for white people to exclude and assert control over minorities. Centuries of a rigged playing field has led to the segregated housing issues that we face today. The saturation of filthy politics and pitiful real estate games has clouded the vision of many to see the privileges white people embrace every day. We have made progress from the 1950's but our new color blind society has led us to a plateau of resolution to a better and equal living quality for all.

Urbanization and its suppression on race equality has resulted in such drastic impact that we still see segregation in our cities today. To find change we have to identify the issues, suburbanization was one of those issues, and embrace the idea of ways to help minorities experience life with the same opportunities white males have had, then just maybe we will live in a better society that benefits us all.

RIGHTING THE WRONGS OF RACISM

Much has been said over the years in relation to slavery and the white man's role in it. What part, if any do white people today have to play in this historical injustice and is there any responsibility to be shouldered in relation to the treatment of black people who suffered for several centuries under this system of servitude?

This is a question that many are uncomfortable with because it engenders a lot of emotion ranging from bitterness to confusion, and to outright rejection. In order to right the wrong of racism, however, it is a question that must be asked and there must be an answer that satisfies both the heart and the mind of those who are either consciously or unconsciously affected by this unfortunate legacy.

The only way to begin to clear the air of this unresolved issue is to deal with it honestly. Yes, slavery in the United States has long since passed into the annals of history but the mental offspring from the minds of those that created such an institution still live on to varying degrees in the ideas and beliefs that many still hold and that affect both their private realities and the public life of our nation.

Naturally, no one alive today can be held responsible for what happened many years ago, but the culpability for those crimes can be said to be the mental step-children of the perpetrators of those acts that have been passed down, in a second-handed fashion to those who still hold the same ideas today.

Some might say that racism and slavery are two different things, yet it is the ideas and beliefs behind racism that created such an institution to begin with, so both concepts are intertwined, one within the other. Those that are most affected by racism in their lives are those who hold many of the same notions that existed a hundred years ago and more.

Many feel a sense of shame and guilt for harboring such ideas and are uncomfortable with themselves for doing so. They may speak of racial inequality and injustice and pay lip service to it but a part of them still believes that blacks are dangerous, inferior, uncivilized, sexually unrestrained and exhibit the darker impulses of man. We can see this belief system operating even in many of the founding fathers of our nation who were considered some of the most enlightened thinkers of that time. Thomas Jefferson, for example, for all his genius, believed that blacks were inferior to whites but at the same time condemned slavery. Why is this? Try as people might, many still hold two conflicting sets of beliefs that keep this issue alive and that unfortunately block the progress and growth of individuals, communities and nations alike.

Most individuals want to believe that all people are equal. What is it then that stops people from following through with that belief and living it in their daily lives? If we look at beliefs as if they were planetary systems we would see that one core belief, or one planet has several other moons or beliefs that rotate around it. These would be called subsidiary beliefs or secondary planets. Often times one of a planet's moons is in the direct orbiting path of another and blocks it from the main planet's 'view.' So the same is true of a core belief. Other subsidiary beliefs rotate around it and often cannot be seen from the main belief's viewpoint, rendering it invisible. Its effects, however, are hardly so.

If a person believes, for example, that all men are created equal, yet at the same time believes that a part of man has an animal instinct that is itself dangerous, and if let free would cause ruin and havoc in society, then he would try to control this uncivilized impulse and repress it as much as he could. And what if this same person cannot accept such a 'darker' impulse within his own mind and instead projects it outward onto another person or race that seems to him to embody such a nature?

Many whites fear blacks because they believe so strongly in the unacceptable darker impulses of their own natures, and that they must hold these sinister aspects of their own minds and souls down at all costs. Blacks became the scapegoat of the denied 'darker' impulses of the white man's ideas of good and evil. Many blacks conversely have unconsciously bought into or have been conditioned by the same set of ideas and act them out in society unknowingly. In other words, value judgments on color have been placed where they don't belong.

There has been a grave error committed and it continues to generate misunderstanding, bitterness, divisiveness and a lack of growth. This error can be called the 'white ethic' and it was given birth centuries ago by individuals who believed firmly in the 'black and white' or 'good and evil' aspects of the mind. These concepts have been unexamined for centuries and they still continue to be an invisible force in the life of many cultures and societies on the face of the earth. It is our beliefs about the inner contents of the mind, projected outward into the world of events that have created racism and the institutions that are a result of this thinking.

To right the wrong of racism the ideas that have given it birth must be changed. To do this requires a new examination, both personally and en masse, into the ideas that we hold not only about race, but also in those beliefs that lie 'hidden' behind racism and are blocked from view by the core beliefs that we hold about good and evil and the nature of the min . Is it an accident, for example, especially in the Western world, that racism and man's concepts of the Devil and the reality of evil as a manifestation of a supernatural force are not nearly as strong as they were, say, 50 or 100 years ago or more? This is not to say that concepts of good and evil are the only factors in this equation, but they cannot be ignored and swept under the rug as if they didn't exist. Ideas of associating evil with darkness and white with goodness may be simplistic, but for centuries man has been guilty of doing just such a thing.

How could a civilized people, building a nation in the 18th and 19th centuries and before capture and enslave another group of people simply because of skin color? The answer to this question is a similar one that can be asked of Hitler's Germany. Why did Hitler and many of the German people take part in and acquiesce to the genocide of the Jews? In this case it wasn't the darker skin color that stamped the Jews with the Scarlet Letter of racial inferiority-it was the rigid ideas of good and evil held by those living at the time that created such a catastrophe. "The evil must be plucked out" was the justifiable idea that circulated in that time and place.

Those who held this concept felt that they were pursuing the good. Otherwise they couldn't have taken those actions. The Jews became the scapegoat for Germany's problems because they were considered to be inferior and the embodiment of evil. Sadly, this same set of beliefs is the root cause of many of the world's problems, both historically speaking and in the context of the present times.

How can man be so cruel to other men? Unfortunately, highly distorted ideas of good and evil are to blame. The men and women who hold them must take responsibility, but let us not blame human nature for these ignominious deeds. It is not human nature that is at fault. It is our ideas and beliefs about human nature and our medieval concepts of good and evil that are in error.

White guilt, as it pertains to racism is the result of two simultaneously held belief systems that have not been reconciled. One says that all men are created equal and the other says that they are not. Until these ideas are exposed, examined and altered they will continue to hold an invisible and 'gravitational effect' upon the minds of many and they will generate events, both privately and in the public arena that reflect these conflicting views.

THE RACE AND RACIST GAME

"The poor should not have a floor and the rich should not have a roof" Race is an idea that early European "scientist" coined to categorize differences in appearance in peoples living in other parts of the world distant from their own. Race began, therefore, as a geographically derived concept. Later, some scientists began to speculate about a hierarchy of capacity or worth associated with various "races" Experiments were conducted to try and prove or disprove differences in human ability linked to perceived race or appearance with predictable results. Whether due to error, bias, arrogance, fear of the unknown and or deliberate act of misrepresentation of history, Europeans scientists concluded that their racial group was "superior" to all others. The notion of american or "white" racial superiority furnished a ready excuse or justification for imperialism, colonialism, conquest and abuse. Yet before the Europeans left their caves in Europe, others such as the Africans, were highly advanced and civilized. It was their interactions with these people that the Europeans were civilized and taught the modern ways of those times.

What is disheartening in America is that many policy makers and so-called analysts spend their time arguing about "racial discrimination" is a problem, when clearly America operate in diverse combination to foster inequality. Debate on these propositions provides a ready excuse for some to decline to support any response to racial discrimination, injustice and inequality.

In the new global economic era, racism and discrimination are no longer functional. At earlier stages of history, having large numbers of poor and uneducated people of African descent to exploit as source of cheap labor may have been beneficial to elite group. This is no longer the case, people around the world are too aware of the reality of racial plight and will not stand or support the old ways anymore. They are quietly fighting the atrocities of racism and unfortunately, Africans don't harbor such hatred toward Europeans in Africa.

In a real sense, discrimination and racism are out-of-date. They have outlived their economic utility. No nation can any longer "afford" to waste the talent and productivity capabilities represented by large African and African American populations. In the highly charged, global marketplace, nations with large numbers of people who are uncared for, unemployed or under employed, undereducated, unskilled and impoverished are a decided disadvantage.

In the past, racism and discrimination may have been a way to enrich members of the population. In the future, racism and discrimination will increasingly hamper the ability of America to achieve or sustain economic growth and development for the benefit of all her people.

Racism and discrimination; no matter how they are explained or characterized are violation of human rights, and it is also violation of both domestic and international law.

Racism and discrimination are not simply matters of interpersonal relations or harmless aesthetic preferences or just habits of the hearts.

They are encoded in institutional policies, practices and arrangement that disadvantage one group unfairly and disproportionately based on race or color and privilege another due to color or race.

In 1946, then acting secretary of states Dean Acheson stated: "the existence of discrimination against minority group in this country has an adverse effect upon our relations with other countries. We are reminded over and over by some foreign newspapers and spokesmen that our treatment of various minorities leaves much to be desired. While sometimes these pronouncements are exaggerated and unjustified, they all too frequently point with accuracy to some form of discrimination because of race, creed, color, or national origin.

Frequently, we find it next to impossible to formulate a satisfactory answer to our critics in other countries, the gap between the things we stand for in principles and the facts of a particular situation may be too wide to be bridge. An atmosphere of suspicion and resentment in a country over the way a minority is being treated in the United States is formidable obstacle to the development of mutual understanding and trust between the two countries. We will have a better international relations when these reasons for suspicion resentment have been removed"

Even worse, the fiction that skin color matters, that it is a legitimate distinction among people, that it signifies a lesser degree of humanity, was created and maintained. Over the years, that fiction became embedded in the American social and political structures. It established and nourished sharp limits on opportunity and therefore on achievement.

One of the biggest mistake made by American policies is not aligning African Americans in the economic fabric of this country, instead they developed foreign markets, versus developing the African American markets at home. Like cancer, the fiction that skin color is a substitute for talent, character, intelligence, and humanity spread throughout the body politic, seeped below the surface of American professed ideals and corroded them from within.

Since white and blacks start off at different points on the scale in terms of resources, power and well-being, undoing the effects of racism and discrimination may require compensatory efforts in order to create parity in the abilities of the two groups to take advantage of "equal opportunities", whites being privileged and blacks not.

If human beings can accept that the earth is round, although our eyes tell us otherwise, why do some people continue to think of themselves and act as it they are "superior" to people of African descent and other minorities or appearance despite overwhelming evidence to the contrary?

Here are some commonly cited reasons for this foolishness of been superior to others and the non-so-called whites.

1. Some people are plain ignorant

2. Other people confuse the degree of development of Europeans or "white" nations with "superiority", without considering the role of European colonialism and slavery in retarding African developments.

3. Isolation and unfounded fears help perpetuate racial stereotypes and distrust of persons perceived to be "different" from one's self or kin.

4. Some people believe that groups differentials between blacks and whites on standardized test performance measure "nature" or characteristics intrinsic to "race, rather than "nature"

5. Confusing poverty and lack of education with lack of intelligence is a common falling

6. Whites who care about fairness but treat others unfairly often cannot face up to what they have done.

7. Perhaps the most powerful reason racism persists is simply that many whites find a belief in the inferiority of blacks useful or convenient.

8. Equating racism and discrimination to the GNP of person's nationality.

9. Judging based on ones understanding and comprehension of the English language.

10. In a short word, some whites are plain stupid to believe that they are better.

THE EFFECTS OF RACE AND RACISM

Racism is corrosive for a society because it teaches people to make judgments about others on the basis of the way they look or assumptions that they might make about people from different cultures. Racism allows people to justify all sorts of indignities and horrors to be visited on people from other cultures by saying that the other people are inferior or somehow less than human in some way.

Effects of Race on Economics

The economy consists of an elite and everyone else. At times 'everyone else' has been stronger relative to the elite, at times weaker. The elite by definition has power over the rest. But the economy is not so simple-- there are some who are more elite and have more power, some who are less. Economic power is a combination of wealth, income, status and occupation, access to education and health care, connections, and geographic and social mobility. These in turn translate into political power, organization, access to media, business and government. A great deal of the damage done by racism is done through the economic system. People of colour are denied economic power, here and in many places in the world. Having economic power or elite status is being in an exclusive club.

How important is race in deciding who gets into this club? Some examples: blacks search for work longer and often more aggressively than whites and are 36-44% less likely to be hired for jobs in mostly white suburbs even when they are just as qualified. White males with a high school diploma are as likely to have a job and earn as much as black males with college degrees. When controlling for age, experience, and other relative factors, blacks are paid at least 10% less than whites. On average, African Americans have only one- tenth the net worth that white Americans do.

People with power do not give it away out of morality or a sense of justice. Instead they use the means at their disposal to maintain and extend their power. They hand out jobs and positions in society, and so have the power to discriminate based on race (and sex) and create the kind of pyramid they want.

The consequences for the economy are these: not only does racism cause the economy to be stratified as it is, and place people of colour at the bottom of the economic pyramid in terms of occupation, empowerment, income, and wealth. Racism also splits the 'everyone else' into racial groups with different interests, and helps elites maintain their economic power against a divided opposition.

We have a society divided by class: what I would call two classes of winners (owners and managers) and one class of losers (workers, including the unemployed)-- others might cut this finer, others rougher.

Most of the winners are white, but most white people aren't winners, at least in the economy. But what we also have is a society divided by race-- where the upper caste is white, and all whites are racial winners-- even those who are economic losers. This scheme of things suits white economic elites-- who create and maintain the scheme by discrimination-- just fine. Racial privilege, in terms of status, prestige, and separation, is much cheaper for them to give out than economic justice, full employment at empowering work, and equality.

When white workers are suffering, people of colour offer convenient scapegoats for structural economic problems: overpopulation is to blame instead of corporate destruction of resources, immigration is to blame instead of deliberate technological unemployment. The presence of more desperate, disempowered people of colour below white workers on the class ladder acts as both a consolation and a discipline. If white workers saw their interests with other workers regardless of race, instead of with other whites regardless of class, it would be more difficult for elites to prevent economic reforms that ended poverty, unemployment, environmental destruction.

In the meantime, the economy wreaks havoc on all but a very few, and worse havoc on those without the insulations of caste privilege.

Equality is incompatible with racism. Democracy, which is people having a say in their government to the degree they're affected by decisions, is incompatible with racism. White workers will never have the bargaining strength they need to have economic security if they choose to accept the divisions that ensue. This is obvious even by a quick glance at the US and Canada. Canada has universal health care and much more progressive taxation and a viable third party—these are all under attack and being dismantled, but they were won in the first place because of working people's fighting and struggling to win them. The US had its own labour struggles where much was won—but labour in the US has always been divided between fighting owners and managers on the one hand, and bashing Black Americans and immigrants on the other. Workers in Canada, virtually the same as the US in most ways but lacking the history of slavery, could focus more on their economic interests and win more. But all this discussion of racism's integral role in maintaining economic inequality and insecurity in the US obscures the tragedy of a racist economy—an economy that wastes human potential and condemns huge numbers to misery and poverty out of spite and cruelty.

WHAT'S SO 'SYSTEMIC' ABOUT IT?

The reason 'racist economics' is so insidious is because it yields racist outcomes even if people are not particularly prejudiced. It is insidious because it makes it possible for the failure of an agricultural program or a race riot decades ago to have an impact on people's economic situations today.

Wealth is passed from one generation to the next. This means that if, in previous generations, black people or native people had no wealth or had it stolen from them, they will have less now than whites. This has all the potential in the world to perpetuate itself.

Jobs and other business opportunities are often not advertised and go instead according to personal and family connections. Even without severe discrimination, in a racist society people have mostly friends and family of their own race. If the people with jobs and opportunities to give out are white, the people who get the jobs and opportunities will be white. This, too, has a self-perpetuating logic. Some specific examples are given below.

Five interactions of racism and economics:

1. Globalization

The interaction of racism and class divisions and its effects are apparent in the context of 'globalization'. Globalization means, in shorthand, that the rich can take their money anywhere in the worl whenever they want. What you as a worker have to understand about this is that if investors or corporations can move plants and headquarters like this, so long as there is anyone in the world who is more desperate than you and willing to work for less, then you cannot have economic security, you cannot make plans for your future or your family, you cannot be sure of a job tomorrow. If white North America workers do not appreciate this, it's because corporations try so hard to spread the word that what's good for North American corporations is what's good for North Americans and that foreign workers are not potential allies but rivals. What happens as a result is shown by a headline in the Globe and Mail in 1997, referring to the destruction of the Asian economies which led to much desperation, misery, and concentration of economic power in elite hands: 'Asian heads bow to global economy'.

2. Closing doors and the army

One principle of racist economics is this: if a job can be given to a white person, all things being equal, it will be. This means that black and Latino youths, especially in hard economic times, have most economic doors closed to them. One of the few that remains open is the military. Military spending is the largest item in the US budget, and is more than social expenditures. Communities of colour are targeted specifically for recruitment, especially poor communities and especially in economic downturns. Recruiters are therefore taking advantage of racially exacerbated economic desperation to recruit people into the army. The result is that the US army, an instrument used to fight wars that are never in the interests of people of colour, usually against countries in Asia, Africa, or Latin America, has an officer corps that is 3% Latino, while casualties tallied on the Washington Monument for example were 28% Latino.

3. Unemployment

The problem of unemployment deserves special mention here. Unemployment is wasted human potential, a horrible allocation of resources, a human tragedy, and a huge obstacle in the way of any kind of change in the economy.

But if it's so bad, why does it exist? You'll hear many justifications from economists. The most famous are:

1. If everyone was employed, they'd all have money and want to buy things, so everyone bidding for these things would cause prices to go up and up, the money wouldn't be worth anything and workers would suffer anyway. This theory says there's a 'natural non accelerating inflation rate of un-employment' above which we can't go. This is an elaborate story with lots of evidence against it, and no evidence for it.

2. The unemployed are unemployed because workers' stand-ards are too high-- if workers would work for less, there would be no unemployment. The limit of this scenario is slavery-- everyone is employed, no one gets paid. My own answer to this is I'll believe that when owners give up all their profits and managers accept the same low (or zero?) salaries as their workers. Until then, I'll think this idea is what it is-- mean ideology pretending to be scientific economics.

3. A more convincing reason for the existence of unemployment is that it's good for elites, and elites won't change what's good for them.

If there was full employment, management would no longer have the threat to fire and replace workers, workers could demand more money, more control over their work and the company's decisions, and actually win them. This would be bad for elites-- unemployment is better.

So unemployment is a matter of deliberate policy. In a racist society, the burden of unemployment will fall hardest on people of colour—the unemployment rate for blacks was 14% in 1992, while for whites it's 6%, What does this mean? The unemployed lack political clout, access to health care, good housing, and nutrition; they are vulnerable to use as strikebreakers. Chronic, long-term, racially-influenced unemployment creates a permanently unemployable class. These unemployed are not even required by the elite to be unemployed-- they're completely superfluous. As a result, they're imprisoned for trivial offenses, locked into ghettos and reserves in appalling conditions.

4. Third World Poverty, Western Foreign Policy, and Immigration Ecologists like Paul Ehrlich, who advocate 'zero population growth', and argue that North America and Europe must remain an 'island of plenty in a sea of despair', have a position easy to fit in with racism.

Indeed the environmental movement is at its most confused when dealing with issues like population, immigration, and poverty. Is overpopulation in the 3rd world causing environmental destruction? Should the 3rd world be kept in poverty out of fear that if 'they' consumed as we did, the earth couldn't survive? Should 'we' restrict immigration to maintain our lands at a level of ecological integrity? The questions themselves betray a misunderstanding about the relationship between the first and third worlds. Population is not a cause but an effect-- of disempowered females who are not allowed to participate in society or the workforce, of poverty and insecurity. People who want to immigrate do so not because of 'population pressure' but because of poverty. Poverty itself is not a consequence of population but of injustice. It is worth describing the cycle of poverty of 3rd world countries in detail It begins with a Western Intervention. This intervention re-orients the economy from self-sufficient agriculture and industry to serve local markets to export-oriented agriculture and no industry. This is done by violence, debt, and bribing local elites. The new agriculture is more productive-- not that it produces more, but it produces different goods (goods the people who grow it can't eat, usually) using less labour. What happens to the agriculturalists who are no longer needed? They go to the cities, places like Mexico City, Bombay, and Jakarta, where they are now the most competitive labour force around (meaning they'll work for really cheap) because they have no bargaining power.

Western corporations are more than happy to 'invest' in such places, and leave if the situation changes. This situation is a horror for the citizens of most of the world, and a joy for corporations. Every third-worlder who can escape from this does their best to do so. If in a country workers begin to organize themselves, or peasants begin to agitate for land reforms, or a government promising to make these changes comes to power, that country is immediately targeted for attack. First, come bribes, media campaigns, and subversions of the military. Possibly mercenaries are employed. If the people of the country keep resisting, they're bombed.

Discussions of 'population' and 'immigration' that obscure this relationship are outrageous. I'm tempted to offer a trade: return every scrap of property held by western corporations in the third world. Dismantle the CIA and the US navy, airforce, and army . Cancel all debts owed to western countries and banks. Dismantle the IMF and the World Bank. Give the third world ten years of commodity prices that reflect the social cost of production of the commodities plus a reasonable profit. Watch as the corrupt elites of the third world are removed from power, land reforms are enacted, and economies are reoriented. Then, and only then, can North America unhypocritically close the borders and get hysterical about lost jobs, immigration, dilution of society's morals, and so on.

And of course, the flip side of this is that the only reason immigrants are allowed in the country is because they're wanted by corporations, to staff the sweatshops, to work on the farms and in the laundries, to raise elites' children and clean their houses and offices, and sometimes to program their computers.

RACISM INTERVENES TO RESTORE INEQUALITY

A great deal about racist economics can be boiled down to a single rule: When possible, a person of colour must not have anything a white person doesn't have. If elites of colour exist and wield power, there must be white elites who wield more power. If there are whites who are poor, there must be people of colour who are more poor.

More than anything else, this has confounded and will continue to confound any effort to lift people of colour out of poverty, starting with the poorest. To do so would require strong public action, whites would never stand for it: if the government belongs to you, it should not do more for other people than it does for you. Even when public action is not involved, and black or native people succeed economically as individuals, their wealth is destroyed. When remedial actions of any kind start to succeed, racist political interventions, sometimes grassroots, sometimes top-down, step in to restore the economic inequalities.

In conclusion, the summary of the effect of race on economics are as follows;

1) Economic elites who have the power to distribute economic benefits such as jobs, wealth, and credit discriminate against people of colour in America, with the result that people of colour are poorer than whites.

2) The poverty resulting from discrimination at home and inability of white workers to perceive their common interests with people of colour means reduced power for both groups, rendering everyone vulnerable to more severe economic exploitation. This vulnerability means it can be more economical to exploit people of colour in the lowest paid, lowest status, most dangerous work, domestically and internationally.

3) The rule of racist society is that people of colour must not have something whites do not. When even a small group of colour makes limited economic gains, political interventions are made to try to undo these.

Racism promotes class stratification and separation, and puts people in different rungs of an economic ladder. It also separates people physically. The separation of people and control of places is a key element of racism

EFFECTS OF RACE ON POLITICS

We've already seen how economic and cultural power is Concentrated in white hands and used to perpetuate racism through those institutions. This section will discuss how Political power to make and enforce laws and resolve disputes is also concentrated, and how white elites use political power to reproduce racism and extend it on the one hand, and to physically smash any attempt at racial progress on the other.

Police

Police are serious purveyors of physical violence to people of colour. Police violence one of the ugliest and most stark facts of racism. The violence, the fear of violence, is why people of colour force themselves to tolerate indignities heaped on them at work, at school, in the media, in the mall, on the street. They know what happens to someone who rebels (and to many who don't rebel).

How does this happen? How can police act this way? There's a theory of guerrilla warfare that says that the people are the sea and the guerrillas are the fish that swim in the sea. White people are the sea, and the police are the fish, here. Some activists of colour have exhorted the white left to take up arms against the police. I don't know about arms, but I can see why they're so frustrated—they want whites to do something about their own police force! Police have the arms and the training. They have the physical power. But their agenda is set by political elites (who are white) and their power is constrained by the fact that they need the community to obey them and respect their authority. They do not control the press nor do they raise money independently. It should be said, though, that both of these things are changing for the worse, with aggressive police unionism that mounts political campaigns and does raise funds—these are bad trends.

But as of now the police are subject to the economic control and monitoring of the community, in particular the press, and civil political authorities.

The communities that suffer the violence of the police do not control the press nor do they control the economy or the political overseers of the police. And the community that does control these powers, the white community, doesn't care what the police do to people of colour. It doesn't care in part because it doesn't know; recall the geographical and occupational segregation; and it doesn't care because it believes its own myths about crime and people of colour.

These myths are spread by the cultural media, If you believe that crime is on the rise, that more police are the way to stop it, and that people of colour are the criminals, you'll support the police in what they do. If you're a police officer and you hold these beliefs, you're ready to become a racial profiler.

The sea and the fish. Everything is set for police to smash people into their racial roles, in brutal ways. In 1996, a Superior Court judge in New Jersey found that black drivers were 5 times as likely as white drivers to be pulled over by police. In April 1998 two NJ state troopers fired 11 shots into a van with 4 unarmed black and brown males on their way to a basketball clinic. They claimed the van was trying to run them down and that they'd pulled the van over for speeding, detected by a radar gun. The troopers had no radar and witnesses claimed the van was moving too slowly to be a threat. Blacks and Latinos were 77.2% of those searched by police on the NJ turnpike.

The 'Justice' System

But the racism doesn't stop on the streets and highways. Every part of the justice system is filled with it. Judges, lawyers, and white juries ensure that the court system has as disparate an impact as policing.

Recall from the economics section the way racism places fewer people of colour in positions of power by discrimination, concentration of wealth and educational and job opportunities, connections, and income. The educational and occupational process which ends in a job as a lawyer or judge acts in such a way that people of colour who tend to reach these positions have a proven ability to at least tolerate racism and a good chance of believing racist myths about their own people.

At every stage of the justice system, authorities have some discretion in their actions. In an overall context of racism, this discretion invariably gets used to the detriment of people of colour.

Arrests.

Black people are arrested at rates disproportionate to their commission of crimes. Victimization reports, for example, show

35% of women reported raped said their assailant was black, and black rape suspects are 43% of those arrested. In Florida in 1993, police rounded up black males between 15 and 21 in Jefferson county to look for a murder suspect. In 1992, all black men at Oneona College in New York were questioned as suspects in a crime because of their race—college officials provided names and locations of all black male students to police when asked. 29% of those arrested are black, but the US population is about 10% black.

Conviction

Black sentences on weapon and drug charges are 49% longer than for whites and are disproportionately convicted —even officials admit this. In a New Jersey poll, 26% of judges said prosecutors were more likely to insist on more serious charges against minority defendants than whites and 20% said sentences for minorities were more severe.

The Death Penalty

A murderer is 10 times more likely to be sentenced to death for killing a white person than for killing a black person. Even at equal 'brutality', murderers are 4 times more likely to get the death penalty if the victim is white. Prisons.

Prisons are being operated as welfare programs, with small communities aggressively lobbying for them because they want the jobs and incomes. Meanwhile real development, featuring useful goods and services and meaningful work and education is not happening or on the agenda. A prison built for the jobs will be filled, and discretion and racism will ensure its racial composition.

The US also has the honour of being the only country on earth to take away the vote for life from offenders who have finished serving their sentences

Political Campaigns

Between the justice system and vigilantes, racism has the violence it needs to contain its victims. But, like the media, politicians' rhetoric and campaigns keep the racist sea favourable for the justice system's fish to do their work.

These politicians traffic in racism because they think it will get them votes, and it does. But their campaigns and misinformation also help create the context, frame the issues, and set the terms of debate. Hate groups flower when overtly racist politicians are in power

Destroying Racism's Enemies

Dissidents of colour, in America and abroad, have an excellent chance of being jailed or simply murdered by authorities. Even a simple reform like making police stick to their own laws and operate openly would be a huge help.

Foreign Policy

The economic interventions of the IMF, World Bank, WTO, FTAA, and multinational corporations, act to preserve a racist colonial world. But when these fail and are resisted, elites have many political resources to deploy. Economic and ideological support for sympathetic Third World elites against those who would pursue some kind of self-determination starts the process. If those third world nationalists are still successful and popular, they can be vilified in the press through the US's many international media connections.

RACE INEQUALITY IN EDUCATION

In the United States educational inequality is produced on two fronts: within the schools students attend and within the homes they return to after the final bell. White students are more likely to attend schools that are better funded and offer more educational resources opportunities than their peers of color . Schools with higher funding can afford to provide their students with state-of-the-art resources, more advanced placement (AP) courses, and a wider array of extracurricular activities. All of which give their disproportionately white graduates an advantage over students from less well funded schools in the competition for admission to the most prestigious universities. This is a form of inequality that is created by the public policy choices of state and local leaders.

We could choose to fund all schools and students equally, but we don't. However, even if we did equalize the funding of schools, educational inequality would likely persist because of the differences between the resources families have to invest in their child's education. White and Asian American households have higher median incomes than households of color. Affluent families can use these resources to provide additional tutoring, expensive extra-curricular experiences, and ACT/SAT test preparation classes. Furthermore, students from low income families are disproportionately likely to have to deal with food insecurity, high crime neighborhoods, and many other stressors shown to lower academic performance

However, what's important here is how supra-individual factors like the family you were born into, the neighborhood you grew up in, and the policy choices of your elected leaders affect your individual chances of getting into the college of your dreams. Because all of these factors differ across racial lines, this is how racial economic inequality creates racial educational inequality.

The U.S. Isn't Ready to "Move Beyond Affirmative Action" Imagine that two students apply for the last spot at Harvard; one from a well funded school and another from a poorly funded school. If both of those students were the valedictorians of their graduating class and both got perfect scores on the ACT/SAT, who would likely get in and why?

RACE AFFECTS IDENTITY

I think that race effect our identity in the different ways. Some people accept people with different skins but others don't accept them. So when you live in a country with multiracial people it is easier to build your identity with no racial problems. There are schools with mix students and than it is normal for your family and friends to be different. When you grow up in a multicultural society you become tolerant to racial problems and you accept any type of diversity. In this way your identity grows in different way as if you live in a country with hostility to other races.

In that case going to school with separate children can not give you opportunity to know other people, to know their way of living and thinking.

The lack of information gives rise to prejudice and hatred based on ignorance. In many cases this type of hatreds caused a lot of pain and sadness. Many wars started because of insane prejudice based on wrong thinking and manipulating with people ignorance.

To prevent that negative thinking and growing up in a society with racial intolerance people must tend to know different culture, to visit other countries and accept people with different colour of skin.

RACISM IN AMERICA TODAY... WILL IT EVER END?

I do see very clearly that we are all connected, and I truly love and acknowledge every race, every ethnic group, every identity, and every culture that exists in America, on this earth. But I, we, would be lying if we did not also admit that the longest running drama and the single most dysfunctional racial relationship in American history is between White people and Black people. That as long as that dynamic dysfunction exists, there is no way we will ever do right by Native Americans who were the victims of genocide, or ever look at Latino immigrants as anything other than cheap labor and outlaws, or ever view Asians as anything other than the stereotypically quiet and often invisible "model minority." And definitely no way we will ever come to know and understand and feel the humanity of people who are Arab, Middle Eastern, Muslim while the Black-White conundrum continues, excruciatingly, uninterrupted. Stated the way they did in "the old country"— WE'VE HAD AT LEAST three major opportunities in American history to confront and end systematic racism directly, but we merely toyed around with the notion, then backed away.

The first was when the colonies were warring with the mother country, England, for independence. How incredible it would have been if "founding fathers" like George Washington and Thomas Jefferson had seriously and instantly freed their own slaves while declaring in their promissory note "all men are created equal." How incredible if Native Americans were treated with dignity and grace, and a part of the vision, instead of as mortal enemies. How incredible if poor Whites and women of all hues, too, were included in the concept of freedom, justice, and equality? And, my God, how incredible would it have been for those Black slaves, my ancestors, to become free women and free men and free children, to participate, from the very beginning, in the building of what we claim to be a democracy?

The second chance was during the Civil War and its aftermath known as Reconstruction. We who truly know American history know that President Abraham Lincoln was not the great emancipator he is hailed to be. Sometimes he was for slavery and sometimes he was against slavery. And unambiguously his releasing from bondage Blacks in selected states gave the North more men to fight and win the war. You think not? Then Google one of Dr. King's last speeches where he referred to Lincoln as the "great vacillator." But, regardless, Lincoln's Emancipation Proclamation was put forth; he was assassinated yet still there was a flickering hope of a better day as colored folks marched from plantations to liberty. But that long walk to freedom turned out to be fool's gold.

Reconstruction lasted only a dozen years, until The Compromise of 1877 put Rutherford B. Hayes into the presidency, troops protecting the basic rights of Black folks were removed from the South, and an insidious White domestic terrorism—physically, mentally, spiritually—exploded across America for nearly a century.

Blame Black folks for every moral issue in our fair land. Make Black men and Black women the poster children for every bad behavior or crime or social misstep in America. Tell Black folks that voting is a ticket to a better society, and then deny it from them every chance you get, with poll taxes, with voter I.D. laws. Create a perpetual atmosphere of intimidation and fear where Black folks never know if they will be tarred, feathered, hung from trees, lynched, bombed, shot, racially profiled, or choke-holded to death ... simply for being Black ...

It is a minor miracle of Almighty God and heaven that in the midst of that post-Civil War America Blacks were able, under harsh segregation laws, to build homes, own land, create schools of every variety, such as my undergrad Shaw University, and the Great Bethune Cookman University from which I was conferred a Doctor of Divinity degree, set up businesses that met each of their basic needs, and have whole communities, largely separate from White America—because they had no other choice. A minor miracle, too, that as racism reared its dreadful head and destroyed peoples' lives and neighborhoods that there were not more race rebellions, such as Tulsa in 1921, each and every year, across America during the Jim Crow era. When racism and intra-racism are the order of the day, it's very easy to blame the ghetto, the 'hood, or so-called niggers. And it is within that context, now, where we also bear witness to the meanness and venom manifested during the Obama years with a president elected by a rainbow coalition that made some believe, naively, that the United States was at its best: full of empathy and compassion and magically post-racial. Instead, during his term, Barack Obama had received more death threats than any other commander-in-chief in American history; he has been thoroughly disrespected by Congressional members and other elected officials, sometimes to his face; and the "they" we Black folks like to talk about still question Obama's nationality and ethnic origins, his religion, and his loyalty to the country.

One of the chief architects of the Obama birtherism lie perpetrated by the 45th president who can certainly be questioned as to the legitimacy of his election with documented evidence by Speciel Counsel Robert Mueller of Russian interference. A president who began his run the office using race as a dog whistle to white supremacists lying dormant for decades waiting for their "white messiah" to emerge and reignight the repungnant stench of hate based on the color of one's skin or their ethnic origin. Donald J. Trump has clearly revealed that the dream of a post-racial America is just that "a dream."

America is still waiting for the dream of Dr. Martin Luther King Jr. to be manifest where we "will be judged not by the color of our skin, but on the content of our character." America is not ready to meet the test of Dr. King's dream of character assessement, by turning a blind eye to elect a man who is not morally fit or politically assute enough to handle the office of the president.

Protests, rallies, marches should continue to happen as long as racism exists, as long as there is inequality, injustice, and the absence of opportunities for all people. They must. But we also must be conscious of how this racism cancer eats at us, how it destroys us from the inside out, how we must learn the difference between proactive anger and reactionary anger. Proactive anger builds bridges, possibilities, alliances, movements, and, ultimately, love. Reactive anger destroys bridges, breeds dysfunction, and spreads more madness and confusion. Yes, passion is necessary, and we should be angry because of what I have described in this essay, for it is a natural human emotion. But that anger must not become the very hate we say we are against.

For White Americans this means you've got to re-invent yourselves if you are serious about ridding our society of racism. You've got to ask yourself who and what was I before I became White? What does it mean to me to be human, to be a human being, and what, again, am I willing to do, willing to sacrifice, and willing to give up to be a part of this necessary healing process? You must learn to listen to the voices of Black people and other people of color, you must not feel the need, through arrogance or insecurity, to tell us who we are, what we should be thinking or feeling or doing, and you must, with love and respect, understand when we may be hyper-sensitive to race, to racism, given the history and present-day realities of our America. Shutting us down or ignoring us or un-friending us says you do not truly want a conversation, as equals, especially if that conversation makes you uncomfortable.

As for me, I just want to be at peace, I just want to see love in the world; I just want to love and honor myself, who I am, without it being considered an affront or danger to someone else, because of racism, because of hate and ignorance and fear. I do not want to pick up a gun and commit suicide at the door of the Florida statehouse because my demons got the best of me like 23-year-old

#BlackLivesMatter activist MarShawn M. McCarrel II. I do not want my life to end prematurely, at your hands or at mine, and I do not want my life to be in vain, because of what I am as a Black man. I do not want my work for freedom, justice, and equality for all people to kill me, is what I am saying, to destroy me, to render me mute and useless, to myself, or to others. That means I just want to be a whole human being, a free human being, and respected as such. And I just want to live in an America, and on a planet, where I can dream, forever, instead of being tired, irritated, uncomfortable, and scared, forever. To the point that my life will somehow wind up as a nightmare.

THE END